195

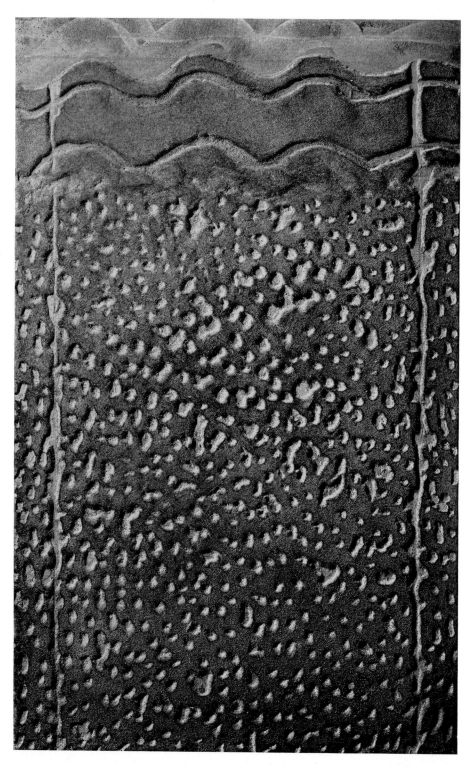

Antoni Tàpies: *Painting*. 1957. Mixed media on canvas, 57⅜″ x 35″. The Museum of Modern Art, New York, gift of G. David Thompson

Frank O'Hara

NEW
SPANISH
PAINTING
AND
SCULPTURE

Rafael Canogar
Eduardo Chillida
Martin Chirino
Modest Cuixart
Francisco Farreras
Luis Feito
Manolo Millares
Lucio (Muñoz)
Oteiza (Jorge de Oteiza Embil)
Manuel Rivera
Antonio Saura
Pablo Serrano
Antonio Suárez
Antoni Tàpies
Joan Josep Tharrats
Manuel Viola

Distributed by Doubleday & Company, Inc., Garden City, New York   The Museum of Modern Art, New York

Library of Congress Catalogue Card No. 60-15021
© The Museum of Modern Art, 1960
11 West 53 Street, New York 19, N. Y.
Printed in the U.S.A. by The Plantin Press, New York
Book design by Charles Oscar

ACKNOWLEDGMENTS

In recent years, visitors to the major international exhibitions such as the São Paulo Bienal and the Venice Biennale have become aware of the vigorous and highly individual work being produced by a considerable number of Spanish artists of the generations following Picasso, Miró and Gonzalez. In the past year or so, European and American museums and art galleries have also begun to show the work of some of these artists. NEW SPANISH PAINTING AND SCULPTURE, however, is the first major survey of the Spanish avant-garde to be presented throughout the United States.

The Museum of Modern Art welcomes the opportunity that this exhibition affords of reciprocating in some degree the generous hospitality of institutions in Spain and the warm response of the Spanish public to American art when our Museum presented MODERN ART IN THE UNITED STATES in Barcelona in 1955 and THE NEW AMERICAN PAINTING in Madrid in 1958. At that time personal contacts were established with many who have been especially active in helping us to realize the present exhibition, which has been planned over a period of more than two years. We acknowledge with special appreciation our debt to Mr. Luis Gonzáles Robles, Chief of Exhibition Services in the Office of Cultural Relations of the Ministry of Foreign Affairs, whose enthusiasm and understanding of the works of his compatriots provided a major inspiration for this project; and to Mr. J. Ainaud de Lasarte, Director of the Art Museums of the City of Barcelona, for his unfailing hospitality and helpfulness. The critical writings of Mr. Juan Eduardo Cirlot, so indispensable for a knowledge of this field, greatly stimulated our interest.

The enthusiastic response of the artists themseves has been a constant incentive, and we are grateful to them not only for their kindness in lending works of art for the exhibition but for encouraging and assisting us in many less tangible ways. Key works were also made available by private collectors and by the artists' representatives, and we acknowledge with thanks the generosity of all the lenders whose names are listed on page 4.

We are especially indebted for assistance to Mr. A. Cirici-Pellicer, Director-designate of the Museo de Arte Contemporáneo now being organized in Barcelona; the collector Mr. René P. Métras; and Mr. Joan Josep Tharrats, with whom The Museum of Modern Art has had contact for many years in his triple capacity as artist, critic and editor of *Dau Al Set*. Mr. Oscar Salvador provided expert guidance through the studios in Madrid, and Mr. John Ashbery of Paris supplied many helpful suggestions that facilitated our work abroad.

Although this exhibition has been organized entirely under private auspices, we have received most cordial and generous cooperation from representatives of the Spanish government both in Spain and in this country. Dr. José Miguel Ruiz Morales, Director General of Cultural Relations at the Ministry of Foreign Affairs has long encouraged the organization of the exhibition and facilitated the arrangements for bringing the loans from Spain to this country. We also encountered unfailing courtesy from Mr. Antonio Espinosa, Cultural Counselor, and Mr. Enrique Suárez de Puga, Second Secretary, Cultural Affairs, at the Embassy in Washington.

Many members of the staff of The Museum of Modern Art have participated in the realization of the exhibition. Its selection demonstrates the insight and critical judgment of its director, Mr. Frank O'Hara of the Department of Circulating Exhibitions. His painstaking research and direct communication with the artists are reflected in the sympathy for their work that is manifested in his stimulating introduction to the catalog. Mrs. Renée Sabatello Neu has ably assisted Mr. O'Hara in research and correspondence. The entire staff of the Department of Circulating Exhibitions has been engaged in the extensive details necessary to prepare the exhibition for its New York showing and to arrange for its subsequent travels throughout the country. And we have, as always, benefited by the wholehearted cooperation of the Museum's Registrar, Miss Dorothy H. Dudley. Mr. Monroe Wheeler, the Museum's Director of Exhibitions and Publications, has provided many invaluable suggestions for the presentation of the exhibition and the preparation of its catalog, for whose production and design we are grateful to Mr. Charles Oscar of the Department of Publications. We are fortunate in having had the benefit of the special knowledge and long interest in this field of the Museum's Librarian, Mr. Bernard Karpel, who has kindly provided the bibliography. Our thanks are also due to Mr. Wilder Green, Assistant Director of the Department of Architecture and Design, who designed the installation for the exhibition's initial showing at The Museum of Modern Art.

We are particularly happy that other cities besides New York will have the opportunity of seeing NEW SPANISH PAINTING AND SCULPTURE, which constitutes the first exhibition to be circulated by The Museum of Modern Art with the aid of a generous grant received from the CBS Foundation for the continuation and strengthening of the Museum's domestic program of traveling shows.

PORTER A. McCRAY
Director, Department of
Circulating Exhibitions

NEW SPANISH PAINTING AND SCULPTURE

Commencing with the appearance of Tàpies, the striking originality and self-sufficiency of whose work placed him very shortly in the foreground of the avant-garde, the number of Spanish artists to attract an international following in the past five years has steadily increased.

Prizes awarded to Oteiza and Cuixart at Bienals in São Paulo, and to Chillida in Venice, have emphasized the emergence of strongly individual talents in the context of what was assumed to be a Spanish School. The recognition accorded Millares, Saura, Rivera, Canogar and others presently made it seem that there was not just one Spanish School, but at least two: the School of Barcelona and the School of Madrid. Whether or not there is this factional hiatus in actuality, reminiscent as it is of the rumored divergence between our own New York School and l'Ecole du Pacifique (a hiatus which, like the Spanish one, was formulated in Parisian critical circles), is a question which seems irrelevant here. The unifying aspect of the activities of these artists is more dominantly characteristic of the present situation.

The isolation of Spain culturally and economically from the period of its tragic civil war until after World War II is well-known. This isolation was not new in Spanish history, and its geniuses did not fail to be heard by the world through one means or another and at whatever cost, even expatriation. But if the most remarkable products of Spanish culture were, in truth, developing apart from their own legacy of cultural vitality, the Spanish expatriates themselves, looking backwards, seem always to have clung to their identification with the Spanish people. France may claim Picasso but Spain, in a sense, owns him.

Many of the artists in the exhibition have spent periods of work or study abroad, but they have also retained close contact with their native land. In great measure, I attribute the vitality of their work, beyond the initial impulse of pure creation, to the desire to provide their society with contemporary values which are neither antiquated, chauvinistic nor sentimental. Each artist must seek the working condition under which he can best function; for those under consideration here it is obviously stimulating to work in Spain, though international honors have exceeded domestic ones. Far from being over-proud of these honors, they seem to consider them a help in bringing contemporary esthetic values to the land of their birth. The latter concern is witnessed by the numerous publications and periodicals with which from time to time almost all these artists have been involved.

The works included in the present exhibition are by no means intended as a comprehensive survey of all the activity going on in Spanish artistic circles today. What is intended is an indication of the diversity of the stylistic tendencies and preoccupations by which some of the leading figures are exploring and developing their individual idioms. They bring to the work itself the excitement of discovery and the vigor of a liberation which has not palled. If it is true, as Sir Herbert Read recently said, that the modern artist is in danger of being cut off from his native cultural roots and thus enfeebled, it is equally true that the artists of certain countries are atrophying from lack of contact with the great cultural movements of contemporary society. It is the latter situation which the activities of these artists are rectifying, even though it cannot be said that their works have gained any widespread popular approval in Spain. No less sophisticated as to means than their colleagues abroad, the "new" Spaniards are frequently less decorative, less chic, more truly elegant, in the sense that elegance involves man's defiance of his logical limitations, and chic the shrewd exploitation of them.

While it is unfortunate that the often remarkable works of earlier periods cannot be represented here, I believe that in most instances those exhibited contain essences of these past explorations. In the studios of Spain the word most frequently heard from artists is "evolution," and the next is probably "organic." Spanish artists do not wish to give up the achievements of the past, or indeed the past itself. They hold tenaciously to values which must be held tenaciously if they are to be held at all, if they are to transform and strengthen a society. The reinvigoration of these values as they have been exposed to the abrasive challenges of esthetic accomplishments and theories from outside Spain has brought about the present period of intense activity and a correspondingly rapid stylistic development in the individual painter and sculptor, a period which seems to have been prophetically initiated by the return to Spain of Miró after World War II.

Living, as Americans do, in an elaborate communications network of public and private galleries and art journals which has continually kept us informed of important events occurring in the other art capitals of the world, it is difficult to imagine the importance which the founding of *Dau Al Set* (Bibl. 22) in Barcelona in 1948 held for the future of contemporary Spanish art. At that time the frontiers of esthetic communication were all but closed to innovation and experimentation. The artists involved in this publication, the painters Tharrats, Ponç, Tàpies, Cuixart, the writers Brossa, Puig, Cirlot, set out to rectify this situation and, what is more important, to give the emerging Spanish avant-garde, few in number at that time, a mouthpiece and a showplace. While the over-all tone was Surrealist, other movements were not neglected, nor was there ignorance of the auras of Picasso, Miró, and Torres-García, among others. But *Dau Al Set* went further, nourishing and stimulating esthetic aspirations beyond the point of influence of any one artist, drawing attention to the medieval masterpieces of Catalan art, as well as to relevant modern masters such as Klee. Not until the founding of the group *El Paso* by Saura, Millares, Canogar and Feito in Madrid in 1957 was there another such historic moment in the development of contemporary Spanish art, though there were in the interim other movements, groups, and alliances of individual artists.

This is not to say that the intellectual life of Spain was at a standstill during this period. But the forms, the ideas, the hopes which, fermenting, invigorate the avant-garde artist, are not necessarily those which attract an educated intellectual in Spain, or for that matter in the United States. To the cultured non-artist they are intangible, they are in the future. To the artist such ideas are meat, they are eminently practical, they are to be absorbed, defended and propounded, or they are to be challenged and combatted. The tradition of *Dau Al Set,* though it ceased publication in the mid-fifties, is continued today by the many Spanish art publications which have followed.

To the widely-dispersed and controversial theories of Action Painting, of the *informel,* of the Absurd, of the Accident, of *art autre,* the artist of each language and each nation brings a correspondingly different interpretation. What makes for these differentiations within an international impulse which is sometimes deplored as uniform, not only throughout the Western world but also in the East? The conscience of a nation, Shelley believed, lies in its artists. Recent history proves him right. Artists of different cultural traditions and present environments cannot simply "take up" the impetus of the international vanguard, any more than their predecessors did in forming it, without severely altering the tempo and the application of that energy. It is to the immediate cultural needs of his society that the modern artist addresses himself. That is precisely what has happened in Spain in the last decade.

The special qualities which Spanish artists have brought to abstract art are several. Already we are aware that the Spanish have challenged certain assumptions which seemed to be safe ones. From Tàpies on, they have tended to question the principles of compositional correctness, particularly in their moral application, and to assume a corrective rather than co-operative stance. In part, their attitude has consisted of an insistence on the literal significance of the plastic means they have used. Rivera, a painter who works in wire and wire-mesh, elaborates his finely drawn configurations without any temptation toward the relief, retaining the flat surface and subtle juxtaposition of tonal effects we encounter in collage and in oil painting. Where there are three dimensional effects, they appear as properties of light and of the material, as in painting, rather than through illusionistic wire volumes. And he himself has not refrained from drawing the analogy between his work and the web of the spider, as a naturalistic hint toward his intentions and the luminosity he has sought so successfully. Tàpies, on the other hand, has moved steadily toward bas-relief. There is no illusion of depth in his recent work, except for the actual depth of gougings and incisions. His insistence on the identity of his material and on the totality of image creates a space into which we do not go: if anything, it advances towards us. We have had much *graffiti* in contemporary painting, but when Tàpies uses them he gives us the wall, too, or a piece of the wall, a relief, a fresco.

Millares, after his earlier periods, began to examine the torn canvas, stitching over the voids, creating harsh and enigmatic encrustations from burlap dipped in whiting, or bandage-like swathes, painted and splattered. Far from being formalistic exercises based on collage, his works have more and more taken on the aspect of ceremonial vestiges, particularly of the bull ring — the elegance of the torero's garments, the torn padding of the horses under the bull's attack. The *homunculi* series presents a specifically figurative development, a far cry from the formal pursuits of Burri, Fontana, Scarpitta, and others who might seem to share similar technical concerns.

Suárez's seeming affinity with the French *tachistes,* the references to Bauhaus and Constructivist geometrical researches in Oteiza's sculpture, the carved surface-depths of Lucio, the freedom of figurative reference in Canogar's powerful action-paintings which proceeds from the subconscious rather than the visual, these are all individual re-interpretations of recognized modern plastic procedures.

It is the Spanish past itself which has led to this cross-pollenation of tradition with contemporary innovation. Picasso, Gonzalez, Miró, the magnificent churches, buildings and parks of Gaudí, the sculptural innovations of Ferrant, all have helped to create a workable *entente* between the past and the present in Spain. But beyond them in time loom the figures of greatness which, as much as its geography, give Spain its special flavor: the Catalan masterpieces in Barcelona; Velazquez and Goya (especially the late Black Paintings of Goya, which have had a pervasive influence); the Roman antiquities and the Roman ruins; the caves of Altamira: all elements which previous Spanish culture had absorbed to an important degree, but which also briefly indicate some of the enthusiasms held by contemporary Spanish artists.

One may find provocative analogies to works of the past in these artists: the circular metallic forms in Cuixart's recent paintings relate to the thick golden halos of fifteenth-century Catalan saints; the *Roots* of Chirino, done in forged iron, are reminiscent of the broken-winged nobility of Zurbaran saints; Saura's *Imaginary Portrait of Goya,* close in its adamant recognition of terror to Goya's own *Dog Buried in the Sand* in the room of Black Paintings in the Prado, a room which contains much that is pertinent to other recent artists, particularly Viola (*The Arrow,* for instance), whose affinity is one of palette rather than iconography. This would be idle speculation were not the actuality of an intensified historical atmosphere present quite tangibly in the works, as well as in the intentions of the artists. Chillida, in carrying on the great tradition of forged iron craftsmanship which is his birthright, is an exemplary figure in that he has also found in the Spanish past the inspiration for his own singular and highly metaphysical expression.

If the motto of American art in recent years can be said to be "Make it new," for the Spanish it is "Make it over." For the authentic heir of a great past the problem is what to do with it, whereas the authentic artist's problem in America is that of bare creation with whatever help from other traditions he can avail himself of. Many constants of Spanish society have remained more or less intact, so that the problems facing Spanish artists today admit of a different solution, but are pressing in the same way as were those of the past. One must remember that the basic idea of the Spanish past has been only fitfully revised, reinterpreted and altered in the light of the dominant movements and ideas of the twentieth century. Past and present are still raw material. This leads to an open, unself-conscious trial of new solutions when they are encountered. Some, developing the absolute image like Tàpies and Chillida, walk the tight-rope between formality and tragedy; others, like Canogar and Millares, plunge ahead into areas of expression where all may be easily lost; others (Rivera, Serrano, Farreras) invite a specific poetry to appear, that of the physical means. Tharrats, the most intellectual, is a headlong expressionist, astral, destructive of order. Feito and Suárez, proceeding through earlier linear and geometric concerns, bring to their different solutions in the one case a tremendously developed instrument of luminous reflectiveness, nostalgic and philosophical, in the other a baroque effulgency of structure related, as much as is the work of Cuixart, to Gaudí.

Despite the enormous stimulus Spanish artists have received from international trends, and from the international art situation into which they were willingly thrust, they remain different, aristocratic, intransigent, articulate. Their activities are prodigious, and it is unfortunate that works of other artists of extraordinary interest could not also be included, such as Alfonso Mier, Carlos Planell, Pablo Palazuelo, Juan Hernandez-Pijuan, Vicente Vela, and the sculptor Subirachs, to name only a few. We will follow the developments of all these artists with the interest which must be accorded artistic ambition and integrity.

FRANK O'HARA
Director of the Exhibition

Rafael
CANOGAR

Rafael Canogar: *Saint Christopher*. 1960. Oil on canvas, 118⅛″ x 78¾″. Lent by the artist

Rafael Canogar: *Painting, Number 56.* 1959. Oil on canvas, 63¾" x 51⅛". Lent by the artist

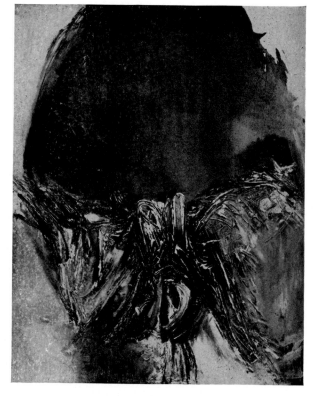

Rafael Canogar: *Painting, Number 57.* 1960. Oil on canvas, 98¾" x 78¾". Lent by the artist

Rafael Canogar: *Toledo*. 1960. Oil on canvas, 98¾″ x 78¾″. Lent by the artist

Eduardo
CHILLIDA

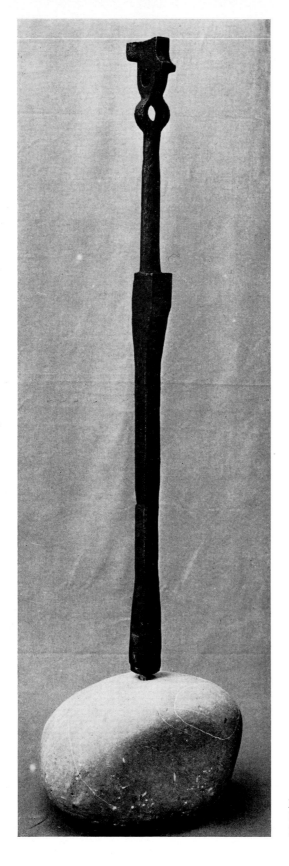

Eduardo Chillida: *Sentinel*. 1954.
Bronze, mounted in stone base, 67¾″
high. Lent by Galerie Maeght, Paris

Eduardo Chillida: *From the Horizon.*
1953. Forged iron, 26⅛″ high. Lent by
Mr. and Mrs. Charles Zadok, New
York

Eduardo Chillida: *Whispering of the Limits, Number 3.* 1959. Forged iron, 25″ high. Lent by Otto Gerson Gallery, N. Y.

Eduardo Chillida: *Place of Silences.*
1958. Forged iron, 15⅝″ high. Lent
anonymously

Martin
CHIRINO

Martin Chirino: *Homage to Julio Gonzales.* 1960. Forged iron, 13¾" high. Lent by the artist

Martin Chirino: *Root, Number 2.* 1960. Forged iron, 13¾" high. Lent by the artist

Martin Chirino: *Root, Number 3.* 1960. Forged iron, 23⅝" high. Lent by the artist

Martin Chirino: *The Wind*. 1960. Forged iron, 7⅞" high. Lent by the artist

Modest
CUIXART

Modest Cuixart: *Painting.* 1959. Oil and metallic paint on canvas, 76¾" x 52". The Museum of Modern Art, gift of Mr. and Mrs. Alex L. Hillman

Modest Cuixart: *Painting.* 1958. Oil and metallic paint on canvas, 51¼″ x 38¼″. Lent by Mr. and Mrs. Alex L. Hillman, New York

Modest Cuixart: *Indulgent Fancy.* 1957. Oil and
metallic paint on canvas, 39½″ x 31¾″. Lent by
Mr. and Mrs. Alexander Lowenthal, Pittsburgh

Modest Cuixart: *Painting.* 1959. Oil and metallic
paint on canvas, 64″ x 51¼″. Lent by Galerie René
Drouin, Paris

Francisco **FARRERAS**

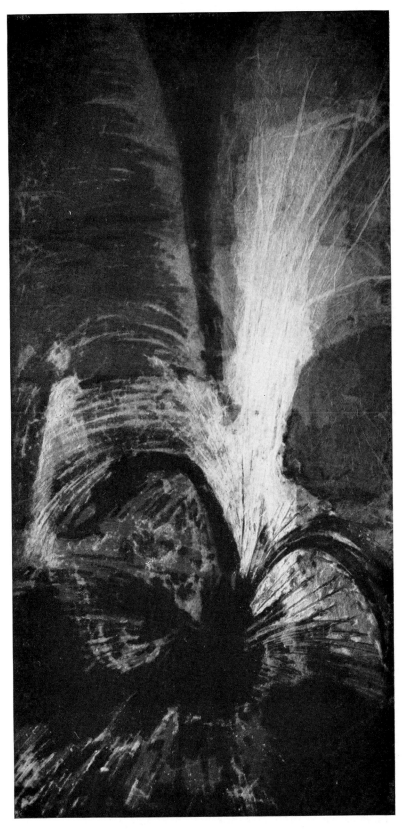

Francisco Farreras: *Number 59*. 1960. Oil and paper on wood (collage). 58¼" x 29½". Lent by the artist

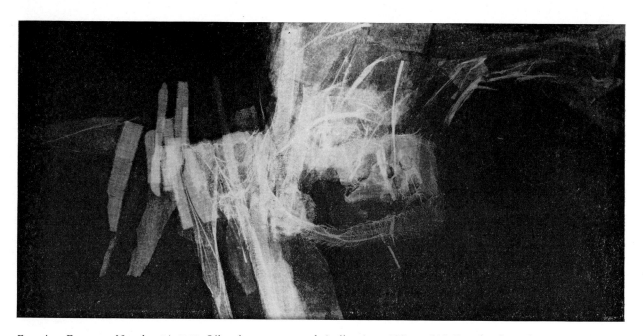

Francisco Farreras: *Number 24.* 1959. Oil and paper on wood (collage), 39⅜" x 78¾". Lent by the artist

Francisco Farreras: *Number 61*. 1960. Oil and paper on wood (collage), 39⅜″ x 58¼″. Lent by the artist

Luis **FEITO**

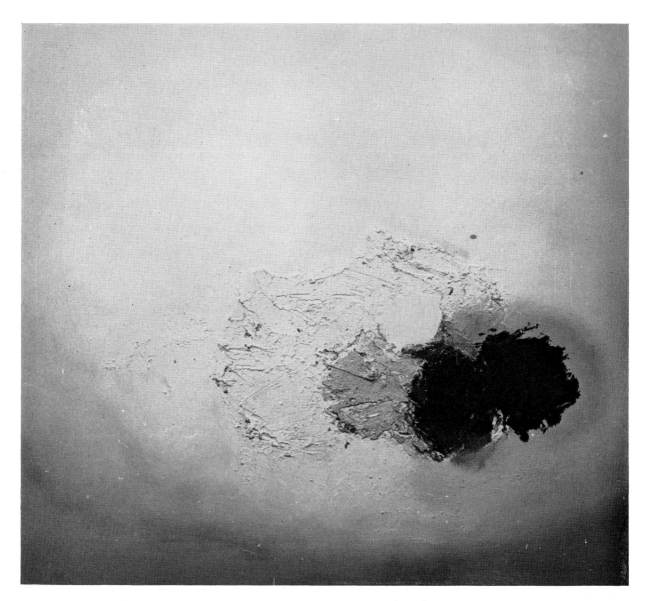

Luis Feito: *Painting, Number 141.* 1959. Oil on canvas, 55⅛″ x 59¼″. Lent by Galerie Arnaud, Paris

Luis Feito: *Painting, Number 147*. 1959. Oil on canvas, 78¾" x 78¾". Lent by Galerie Arnaud, Paris

Luis Feito: *Painting, Number 139*. 1959. Oil on canvas, 44½″ x 57⅜″. Lent by Galerie Arnaud, Paris

Manolo
MILLARES

Manolo Millares: *Homunculus*. 1959. Oil on canvas, 78¾" x 58¼". Lent by Pierre Matisse Gallery, New York

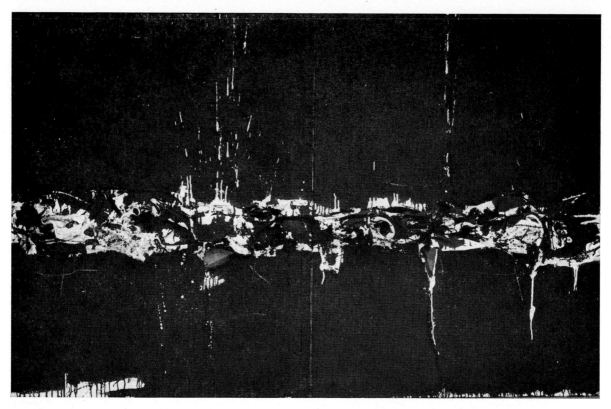

Manolo Millares: *Painting 97*. 1960. Oil on canvas, 63¾" x 102¼". Lent by Pierre Matisse Gallery, New York

Manolo Millares: *Painting 96*. 1960. Oil on canvas, 58¼" x 78¾". Lent by Pierre Matisse Gallery, New York

Manolo Millares: *Homunculus*. 1960. Oil on canvas, 78¾″ x 58¼″. Lent by Pierre Matisse Gallery, New York

LUCIO

(Muñoz)

Lucio (Muñoz): *Wood Painting, Number 6.* 1960. Oil on composition board, 58¼″ x 39⅜″.
Lent by the artist

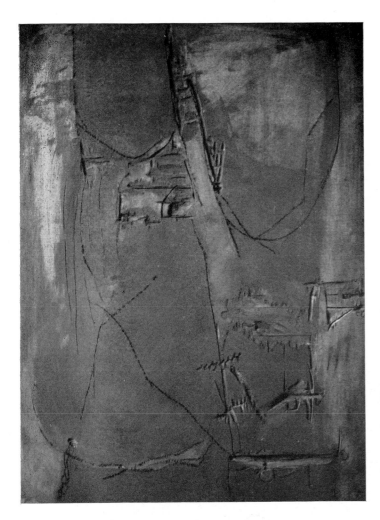

Lucio (Muñoz): *Wood Painting, Number 5.* 1960. Oil on composition board, 51⅛″ x 38⅞″. Lent by the artist

below: Lucio (Muñoz): *Jonas, Number 3.* 1960. Oil on composition board, 39⅜″ x 74¾″. Lent by the artist

OTEIZA

(Jorge de Oteiza Embil)

Oteiza: *Metaphysical Box, Number 1.* 1958. Aluminum, 15¼" high. Lent by Gres Gallery, Washington, D.C.

Oteiza: *Slow Forms before Closing Space.* 1958. Iron, 27½" high. Lent by Gres Gallery, Washington, D.C.

opposite top: Oteiza: *Empty Suspension (Funeral Cortège, Homage to the Aeronautical Engineer, René Couzinet).* 1957. Iron, 21¼" high. Lent by Gres Gallery, Washington, D.C.

opposite bottom: Oteiza: *Dynamic Conjunction of Two Pairs of Light Segments.* 1957. Iron, 13⅜" high. Lent by Gres Gallery, Washington, D.C.

Manuel
RIVERA

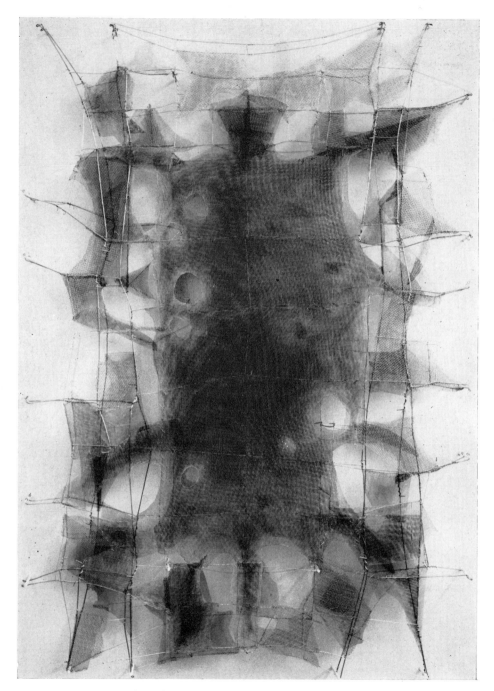

Manuel Rivera: *Metamorphosis (Heraldry)*. 1960. Wire and wire mesh on painted wood, 63¾" x 44⅞". Lent by Pierre Matisse Gallery, New York

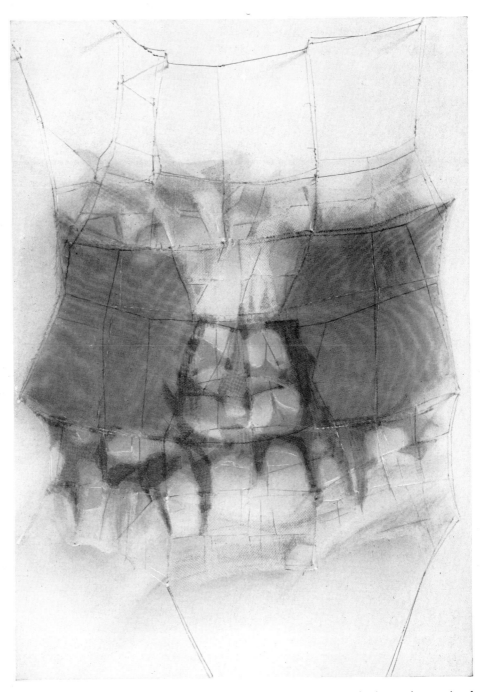

Manuel Rivera: *Metamorphosis (Homage to Bach)*. 1960. Wire and wire mesh on painted wood, 63¾" x 44⅞". Lent by Pierre Matisse Gallery, New York

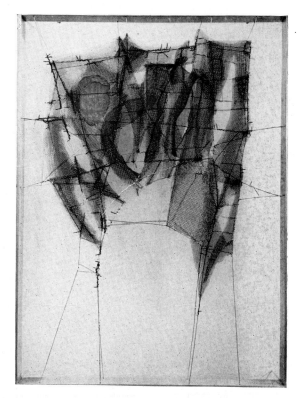

Manuel Rivera: *Metamorphosis (Peddler)*. 1960. Wire and wire mesh on painted wood, 47¼″ x 39¾″. Lent by Pierre Matisse Gallery, New York

Manuel Rivera: *Metamorphosis (Vicente Escudero)*. 1960. Wire and wire mesh in aluminum rectangle, 39⅜″ x 28¾″. Lent by Pierre Matisse Gallery, New York

Antonio **SAURA**

Antonio Saura: *Crucifixion, Number 12.* 1959. Oil on canvas, 78¾" x 98½". Lent by Pierre Matisse Gallery, New York

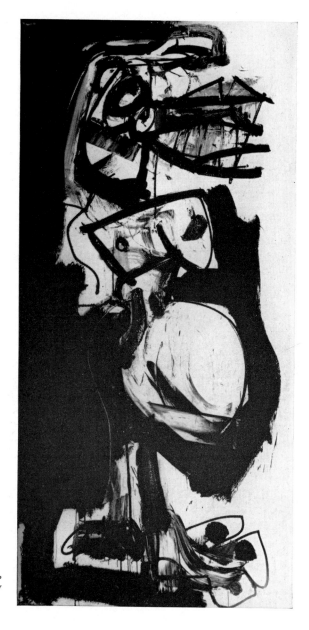

Antonio Saura: *The Three Graces*. 1959. Oil on canvas,
76¾″ x 114¼″. Lent by Pierre Matisse Gallery, New
York

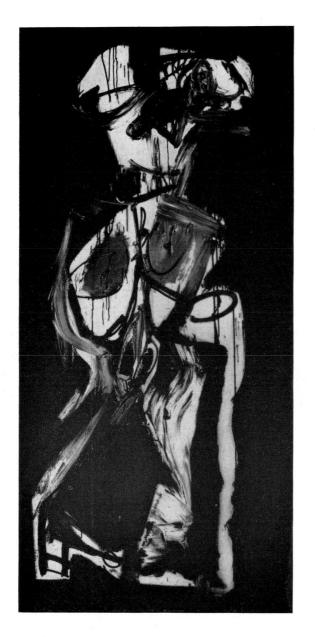
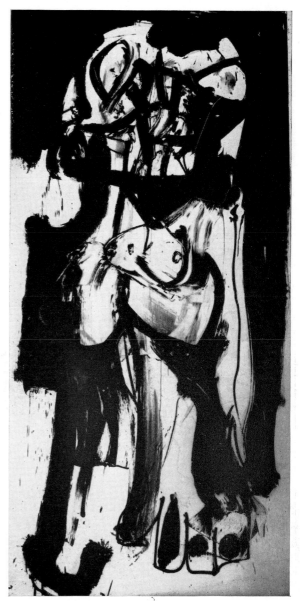

Antonio Saura: *Imaginary Portrait of Goya.* 1959-60. Oil on canvas, 98½" x 78¾". Lent by Pierre Matisse Gallery, New York

Pablo **SERRANO**

Pablo Serrano: *Taurobolium*. 1960. Welded iron, 53⅛″ high. Lent by the artist

Pablo Serrano: *Space*. 1960. Welded iron, 72½″ high. Lent by the artist

Antonio
SUÁREZ

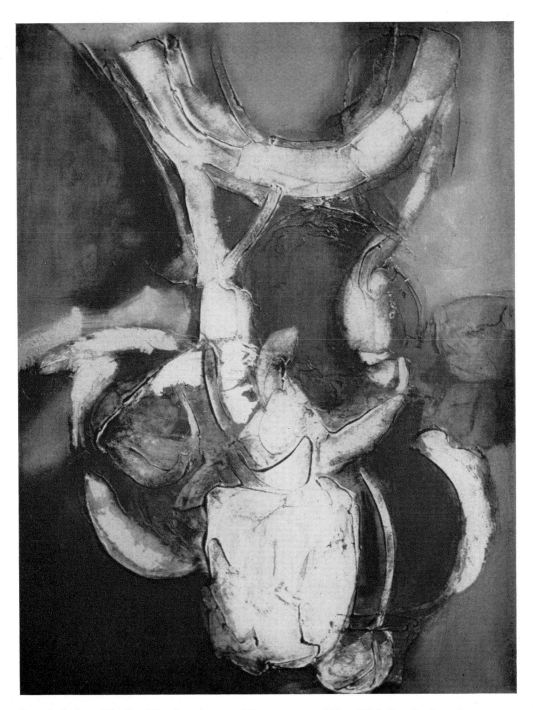

Antonio Suárez: *The Ox (Number 3)*. 1959. Oil on canvas, 57½″ x 44⅞″. Lent by the artist

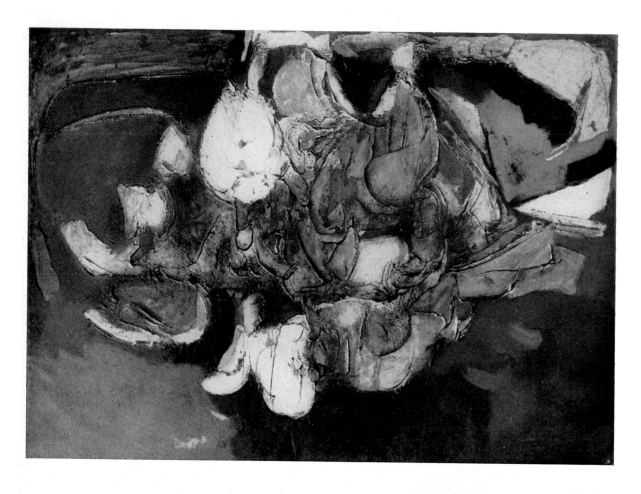

above: Antonio Suárez: *The Fates (Number 1).*
1960. Oil and aluminum paint on canvas, 51⅛″ x
71⅝″. Lent by the artist

Antonio Suárez: *Painting (Number 2).* 1960. Oil
on canvas, 18⅛″ x 13″. Lent by the artist

Antoni
TÀPIES

Antoni Tàpies: *Three Stains on Grey Space.* 1957. Mixed media on canvas, 57½" x 35⅛".
Lent by Miss Isabel C. Raphael, New York

Antoni Tàpies: *Graffiti on Blackish Ochre Relief*. 1957. Mixed media on canvas, 25″ x 32½″. Lent by Mr. and Mrs. Morton G. Neumann, Chicago

Antoni Tàpies: *Space*. 1956. Mixed media on
canvas, 76⅝″ x 67″. The Museum of Modern
Art, gift of Mrs. Martha Jackson

Antoni Tàpies: *Reddish Painting*. 1958.
Mixed media on canvas, 51¼″ x 51¼″. Lent
by Martha Jackson Gallery, New York

Joan Josep **THARRATS**

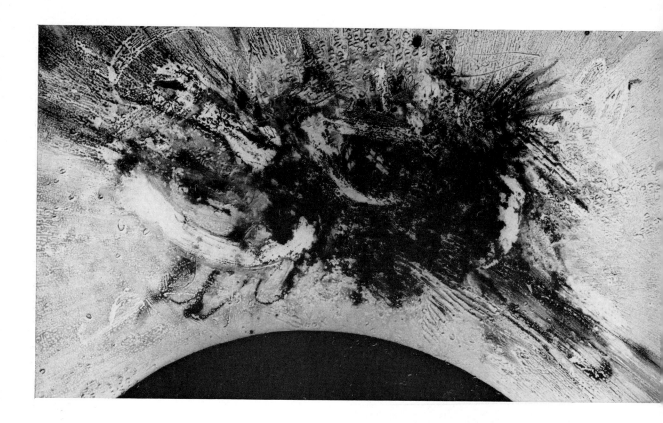

above: Joan Josep Tharrats: *Médamothi.* 1958-60. Oil on canvas, 44⅞″ x 79¾″. Lent by the artist

right: Joan Josep Tharrats: *Sign.* 1959. Oil on canvas, 39⅜″ x 39⅜″. Lent by Rear Admiral Paul Lamar Joachim (U.S.N., retired), Chicago

opposite page: Joan Josep Tharrats: *Homage to Frank Lloyd Wright.* 1959. Oil on canvas, 63¾″ x 51¼″. Lent by Mme Alexis Zalstem-Zalessky, New Milford, Connecticut

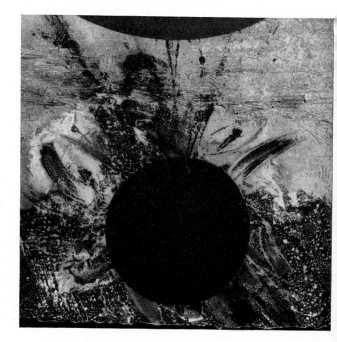

50

Manuel **VIOLA**

Manuel Viola: *The Arrow*. 1958. Oil on canvas, 63¾" x 38⅞". Lent by the artist

Manuel Viola: *Homage to Rothko.* 1959. Oil on canvas, 51¼" x 35¾". Lent by Walter S. Goodhue, Alexandria, Virginia

Rafael Canogar

Eduardo Chillida

Martin Chirino

Modest Cuixart

Francisco Farreras

Luis Feito

Manolo Millares

Lucio (Muñoz)

Oteiza

Manuel Rivera

Antonio Saura

Pablo Serrano

Antonio Suárez

Antoni Tàpies

Joan Josep Tharrats

Manuel Viola

BIOGRAPHIES OF THE ARTISTS AND CATALOG OF THE EXHIBITION

In the listing of measurements for paintings, height precedes width. In the biographical and bibliographical notes where alternate spellings, hyphenations and accents exist, the artist's own preference or the form in most prevalent usage has been followed.

An asterisk preceding the title indicates that the work will be shown in New York only. Two asterisks indicate the work will be shown outside of New York only.

RAFAEL CANOGAR

Painter. Born Toledo, 1934. Studied painting with Daniel Vásquez Diaz, 1948-53. First one-man show, Galería Altamira, Madrid, 1954. First abstract paintings, 1955. First one-man show abroad, Galerie Arnaud, Paris, 1955. Co-founder, with Millares, Saura and Feito of *El Paso* group, in Madrid, 1957; participated in their first group exhibition, Galería Buccholz, the same year. Exhibited in the following international shows: Bienal Hispanoamericana, Madrid, 1951 and Havana (Cuba), 1953; Venice Biennale, 1956, 1958; Pittsburgh Bicentennial International Exhibition of Contemporary Painting and Sculpture, 1958-59; Premio Lissone, Lissone (Italy), 1959; São Paulo Bienal, 1959. Included in *13 peintres espagnols actuels,* Paris, 1959[1] and in *European Art Today,* Minneapolis, 1959.[2] Exhibited with Millares, Rivera, and Saura, Pierre Matisse Gallery, New York, 1960. Lives in Madrid.

Painting, Number 56. 1959. Oil on canvas, 63¾″ x 51⅛″. Lent by the artist. Ill. p. 12

Painting, Number 57. 1960. Oil on canvas, 98¾″ x 78¾″. Lent by the artist. Ill. p. 12

Saint Christopher. 1960. Oil on canvas, 118⅛″ x 78¾″. Lent by the artist. Ill. p. 11

Toledo. 1960. Oil on canvas, 98¾″ x 78¾″. Lent by the artist. Ill. p. 13

EDUARDO CHILLIDA

Sculptor. Born San Sebastian, 1924. Studied architecture, University of Madrid, 1943-47. Began sculpting, 1947. Between 1947-51, lived in Paris. First one-man show, Galería Clan, Madrid, 1954. Among his commissions are four doors for the Basilica of Aranzazu and a monument to Sir Alexander Fleming, San Sebastian, 1955. First one-man show

abroad, Galerie Maeght, Paris, 1956. Awarded $10,000 Graham Foundation Grant for Advanced Studies in Fine Arts, Chicago, 1958. Participated in the following international exhibitions: Triennale, Milan, 1954 (won Diploma of Honor); Venice Biennale, 1958 (won International Prize for Foreign Sculpture); Pittsburgh Bicentennial International Exhibition of Contemporary Painting and Sculpture, 1958-59; Documenta, Kassel, 1959. Seen in the United States in *Sculptures and Drawings from Seven Sculptors,* Solomon R. Guggenheim Museum, New York, 1957 and *European Art Today,* Minneapolis, 1959.[2] Lives in San Sebastian.

From the Horizon. 1953. Forged iron, 26⅛″ high. Lent by Mr. and Mrs. Charles Zadok, New York. Ill. p. 15

Sentinel. 1954. Bronze, mounted in stone base, 67¾″ high. Lent by Galerie Maeght, Paris. Ill. p. 14

Place of Silences. 1958. Forged iron, 15⅝″ high. Lent anonymously. Ill. p. 16

**Whispering of the Limits, Number 3.* 1959. Forged iron, 25″ high. Lent by Otto Gerson Gallery, New York. Ill. p. 16

MARTIN CHIRINO

Sculptor. Born Las Palmas, 1925. Studied at the Escuela de Bellas Artes de San Fernando, Madrid. Traveled to Paris and London where he continued his studies. Returned to Las Palmas and began to experiment with wood, stone, cement and iron in making abstract sculptures. Moved to Madrid, 1955. Member of *El Paso* group. First one-man show Ateneo, Madrid, 1958, also shown in Barcelona. Participated in São Paulo Bienal, 1959. Lives in Madrid.

Homage to Julio Gonzales. 1960. Forged iron, 13¾″ high. Lent by the artist. Ill. p. 17

Root, Number 2. 1960. Forged iron, 13¾″ high. Lent by the artist. Ill. p. 18

Root, Number 3. 1960. Forged iron, 23⅝″ high. Lent by the artist. Ill. p. 18

The Wind. 1960. Forged iron, 7⅞″ high. Lent by the artist. Ill. p. 19

MODEST CUIXART

Painter. Born Barcelona, 1925. Began drawing and painting in watercolor, 1941. In 1944, enrolled in Faculty of Medi-

1 Bibl. 57
2 Bibl. 55
3 Bibl. 51

cine, University of Barcelona. Included in group exhibition the same year and won first prize; in 1946 gave up study of medicine to devote himself to painting. Co-founder, with painters Tharrats, Ponç, and Tàpies and writers Brossa, Puig and Cirlot of the *Dau Al Set* group in Barcelona, 1948. First one-man show, Galerías Sapis, Palma de Mallorca, 1950. In 1951, visited Paris and Lyon. Designed sets for the Guignol Theater in Lyon. On his return to Barcelona the same year, participated in the first official *Dau Al Set* exhibition, Sala Caralt. Traveled to Switzerland and Austria and returned to Paris and Lyon, 1952-55. Participated in the following international shows: Venice Biennale, 1958; Pittsburgh Bicentennial International Exhibition of Painting and Sculpture, 1958-59; Documenta, Kassel, 1959; Premio Lissone, Lissone (Italy), 1959; São Paulo Bienal, 1959 (won Grand Prize). Included in *13 peintres espagnols actuels,* Paris, 1959[1] and *La Nueva Pintura de España,* London, 1960.[3] Lives in Barcelona.

Indulgent Fancy. 1957. Oil and metallic paint on canvas, 39½" x 31¾". Lent by Mr. and Mrs. Alexander Lowenthal, Pittsburgh. Ill. p. 22

Painting. 1958. Oil and metallic paint on canvas, 51¼" x 38¼". Lent by Mr. and Mrs. Alex L. Hillman, New York. Ill. p. 21

*Painting. 1959. Oil and metallic paint on canvas, 76¾" x 52" The Museum of Modern Art, gift of Mr. and Mrs. Alex L. Hillman. Ill. p. 20

Painting. 1959. Oil and metallic paint on canvas, 64" x 51¼". Lent by Galerie René Drouin, Paris. Ill. p. 22

FRANCISCO FARRERAS

Painter. Born Barcelona, 1927. Began study of painting with Gomez Cano of Murcia, 1940. In 1942 went to the Escuela de Artes y Oficios, Tenerife and then to the Escuela de Bellas Artes de San Fernando, Madrid, where he received his diploma. First one-man show, Galerías Biosca, Madrid, 1952. Traveled extensively in Belgium, The Netherlands, England and France. First one-man show abroad, Galerie Vivet, Paris, 1955. First non-figurative works, 1955. In 1956 won competition for thirteen frescoes, chapel of Castillo de Las Navas del Marques, Avila. Designed stained-glass windows for the seminary of the Dominicans, Madrid, and, with the painter Labra, for the Cathedral of Tangiers. Has executed mosaics, frescoes and stained-glass windows in buildings throughout Spain. Participated in the following international exhibitions: Bienal Hispanoamericana, Madrid, 1951, Havana (Cuba), 1953 and Barcelona, 1955; Venice Biennale, 1954, 1958, 1960. Lives in Madrid.

Number 24. 1959. Oil and paper on wood (collage), 39⅜" x 78¾". Lent by the artist. Ill. p. 24

Number 59. 1960. Oil and paper on wood (collage), 58¼" x 29½". Lent by the artist. Ill. p. 23

Number 61. 1960. Oil and paper on wood (collage), 39⅜" x 58¼". Lent by the artist. Ill. p. 25

LUIS FEITO

Painter. Born Madrid, 1929. Studied at the Escuela de Bellas Artes de San Fernando, Madrid; received diploma, 1954. In the same year held first one-man show, Galería Buccholz, Madrid, and, receiving scholarships from both the French and Spanish governments, traveled to Paris. First one-man show abroad, Galerie Arnaud, Paris, 1955. Co-founder, with Canogar, Saura and Millares of *El Paso* group in Madrid, 1957; in same year participated in first *El Paso* group show, Galería Buccholz, Madrid. Participated in the following international exhibitions: Bienal Hispanoamericana, Barcelona, 1955; Biennial of Mediterranean Art, Alexandria (Egypt), 1956 (won prize); Venice Biennale, 1956, 1958, 1960 (won David E. Bright prize); São Paulo Bienal, 1957; Documenta, Kassel, 1959; Premio Lissone, Lissone (Italy), 1959 (won Young International Painting Prize). Included in *13 peintres espagnols actuels,* Paris, 1959[1] and *La Nueva Pintura de España,* London, 1960.[3] First one-man show in the United States, Grace Borgenicht Gallery, New York, 1960. Lives in Madrid.

Painting, Number 139. 1959. Oil on canvas, 44½" x 57⅜". Lent by Galerie Arnaud, Paris. Ill. 28

Painting, Number 141. 1959. Oil on canvas, 55⅛" x 59¼". Lent by Galerie Arnaud, Paris. Ill. p. 26

Painting, Number 147. 1959. Oil on canvas, 78¾" x 78¾". Lent by Galerie Arnaud, Paris. Ill. p. 27

MANOLO MILLARES

Painter. Born Las Palmas, 1926. First painted landscape; turned briefly to surrealism in 1948; by 1949 was experimenting with abstraction. First one-man show, Museo Canario, Las Palmas, 1948. Moved to Madrid, 1955. Co-founder of *Planas de Poesía;* in charge of *Arqueros;* other magazines to which he has contributed are: *Arte Vivo, Problemas de Arte Contemporáneo,* and *Plus.* Co-founder, with Saura, Feito and Canogar of the *El Paso* group, in Madrid, 1957; in the first group show of *El Paso,* Galería Buccholz, Madrid the same year. Participated in the following international exhibitions: Bienal Hispanoamericana, Madrid, 1951, Havana (Cuba), 1953 and Barcelona, 1955; Venice Biennale, 1956, 1958; São Paulo Bienal, 1957; Premio Lissone, Lissone (Italy), 1959. Included in *13 peintres espagnols actuels,* Paris, 1959,[1] and *La Nueva Pintura de España,* London, 1960.[3] In the United States, participated in *European Art Today,* Minneapolis, 1959,[2] *Recent Acquisitions,* The Museum of Modern Art, New York, 1959 and was exhibited with Rivera, Saura and Canogar, Pierre Matisse Gallery, New York, 1960. First one-man show in the United States, Pierre Matisse Gallery, New York, 1960. Lives in Madrid.

Homunculus. 1959. Oil on canvas, 78¾″ x 58¼″. Lent by Pierre Matisse Gallery, New York. Ill. p. 29

Homunculus. 1960. Oil on canvas, 78¾″ x 58¼″. Lent by Pierre Matisse Gallery, New York. Ill. p. 31

Painting 96. 1960. Oil on canvas, 58¼″ x 78¾″. Lent by Pierre Matisse Gallery, New York. Ill. p. 30

Painting 97. 1960. Oil on canvas, 63¾″ x 102¼″. Lent by Pierre Matisse Gallery, New York. Ill. p. 30

LUCIO (MUÑOZ)

Painter. Born Madrid, 1929. Studied at the Escuela de Bellas Artes de San Fernando, Madrid. Spent one year in Paris on a Spanish government scholarship, and has visited England and Italy. First one-man show, Sala de la Direccíon de Bellas Artes, Madrid, 1955. Exhibited in Venice Biennale, 1960. Has participated in several exhibitions in Europe including *13 peintres espagnols actuels,* Paris, 1959,[1] and *La Nueva Pintura de España,* London, 1960.[3] Lives in Madrid.

Jonas, Number 3. 1960. Oil on composition board, 39⅜″ x 74¾″. Lent by the artist. Ill. p. 33

Wood Painting, Number 5. 1960. Oil on composition board, 51⅛″ x 38⅞″. Lent by the artist. Ill. p. 33

Wood Painting, Number 6. 1960. Oil on composition board, 58¼″ x 39⅜″. Lent by the artist. Ill. p. 32

OTEIZA (JORGE DE OTEIZA EMBIL)

Born Orio, province of Guipuzcoa, 1908. Entered the Faculty of Medicine, University of Madrid, 1928. After winning the first prize for sculpture at the Biennial of Guipuzcoa, San Sebastian, in 1931, abandoned medicine to take up sculpture. First one-man show, San Sebastian, 1934. Lived, worked and lectured throughout South America. Among his commissions are sculptures for the Dominican church, Valladolid, 1954. Participated in the following international shows: Triennale, Milan, 1951 (won Honorable Mention); International Sculpture Competition: "The Unknown Political Prisoner," London, 1953; São Paulo Bienal, 1957 (won International Sculpture Prize). Lives in Irun.

Dynamic Conjunction of Two Pairs of Light Segments. 1957. Iron, 13⅜″ high. Lent by Gres Gallery, Washington, D.C. Ill. p. 34

Empty Suspension (Funeral Cortège, Homage to the Aeronautical Engineer, René Couzinet). 1957. Iron, 21¼″ high. Lent by Gres Gallery, Washington, D.C. Ill. p. 34

Metaphysical Box. Number 1. 1958. Aluminum, 15¼″ high. Lent by Gres Gallery, Washington, D.C. Ill. p. 35

Slow Forms before Closing Space. 1958. Iron, 27½″ high. Lent by Gres Gallery, Washington, D.C. Ill. p. 35

MANUEL RIVERA

Painter. Born Granada, 1927. Studied painting at the Escuela de Artes y Oficios, Granada and the Escuela Superior de Santa Isabel de Hungria, Seville. First non-figurative work, 1950. Moved to Madrid, 1951. Joined the *El Paso* group and participated in their first exhibition, Galería Buccholz, Madrid, 1957. Has executed a number of murals in various cities in Spain. First one-man show, Ateneo, Madrid, 1959. Participated in the following international exhibitions: Bienal Hispanoamericana, Madrid, 1951, Havana (Cuba), 1953 and Barcelona, 1955; São Paulo Bienal, 1957; Venice Biennale, 1958; Premio Lissone, Lissone (Italy), 1959 (won Special Mention). Included in *13 peintres espagnols actuels,* Paris, 1959.[1] Exhibited with Millares, Saura, and Canogar, Pierre Matisse Gallery, New York, 1960. Lives in Madrid.

Metamorphosis (Heraldry). 1960. Wire and wire mesh on painted wood, 63¾″ x 44⅞″. Lent by Pierre Matisse Gallery. New York. Ill. p. 36

Metamorphosis (Homage to Bach). 1960. Wire and wire mesh on painted wood, 63¾″ x 44⅞″. Lent by Pierre Matisse Gallery, New York. Ill. p. 37

Metamorphosis (Peddler). 1960. Wire and wire mesh on painted wood, 47¼″ x 39¾″. Lent by Pierre Matisse Gallery, New York. Ill. p. 38

Metamorphosis (Vicente Escudero). 1960. Wire and wire mesh in aluminum rectangle, 39⅜″ x 28¾″. Lent by Pierre Matisse Gallery, New York. Ill. p. 38

ANTONIO SAURA

Painter. Born Huesca, 1930. Taught himself to paint in 1947 after a long illness. First one-man show of early surrealistic work, Galería Buccholz, Madrid, 1951-52. Lived in Paris, 1953-55, where he began experimenting with abstract expressionism. Returned to Spain, and with Millares, Feito and Canogar, founded the *El Paso* group in Madrid, 1957; participated in their first group exhibition the same year, Galería Buccholz, Madrid. Shown in the following international exhibitions: Venice Biennale, 1956, 1958; Pittsburgh Bicentennial International Exhibition of Painting and Sculpture, 1958-59; Documenta, Kassel, 1959; Premio Lissone, Lissone (Italy), 1959; Vitalità nell'Arte, Venice, Recklinghausen, Amsterdam, 1959-60. First one-man show abroad, Galerie Stadler, Paris, 1959. Included in *13 peintres espagnols actuels,* Paris, 1959[1] and *La Nueva Pintura de España,* London, 1960.[3] In the United States exhibited in *European Art Today,* Minneapolis, 1959,[2] and with Millares, Canogar and Rivera, Pierre Matisse Gallery, New York, 1960. Lives in Madrid.

Crucifixion, Number 12. 1959. Oil on canvas, 78¾″ x 98½″. Lent by Pierre Matisse Gallery, New York. Ill. p. 39

The Three Graces. 1959. Oil on canvas, 76¾″ x 114¼″. Lent by Pierre Matisse Gallery, New York. Ill. p. 40-41

Imaginary Portrait of Goya. 1959-60. Oil on canvas, 98½″ x 78¾″. Lent by Pierre Matisse Gallery, New York. Ill. p. 42

PABLO SERRANO

Sculptor. Born Crivellán, province of Teruel, 1910. Studied Barcelona, 1922. Began sculpting, 1928. Moved to Montevideo, Uruguay, 1930. First style academic, became more expressionistic in 1940. In 1946, under the influence of Torres-García, began experimenting with abstraction. Numerous commissions in Uruguay. Returned to Spain, 1955. Traveled extensively in Europe, 1956. Joined *El Paso* group, 1957, and participated in their first group exhibition, Galería Buccholz, Madrid the same year. Broke away from *El Paso* in 1958 and continues working independently. Went to Paris, 1958. Participated in the following international shows: International Sculpture Competition, "The Unknown Political Prisoner," London, 1953 (for Uruguay); Bienal Hispanoamericana, Barcelona, 1955. Lives in Madrid.

Space. 1960. Welded iron, 72½″ high. Lent by the artist. Ill. p. 44

Taurobolium. 1960. Welded iron, 53⅛″ high. Lent by the artist. Ill. p. 43

ANTONIO SUÁREZ

Painter. Born Gijón, 1923. First one-man show, Sala Cristamol, Gijón, 1947. 1950, moved to Madrid. The same year, went to Paris, where he stayed until 1953. First one-man show abroad, Galerie Vidal, Paris, 1952. Returned to Spain, where he collaborated with architects in executing murals, mosaics and stained-glass windows for private and public buildings. In 1955, received traveling fellowship. Participated in first *El Paso* group exhibition, Galeria Buccholz, Madrid, 1957. Included in the following international exhibitions: Biennial of Mediterranean Art, Alexandria (Egypt), 1957; Venice Biennale, 1958; São Paulo Bienal, 1959. Also in *13 peintres espagnols actuels,* Paris, 1959.[1] Lives in Madrid.

The Ox (Number 3). 1959. Oil on canvas, 57½″ x 44⅞″. Lent by the artist. Ill. p. 45

The Fates (Number 1). 1960. Oil and aluminum paint on canvas, 51⅛″ x 71⅝″. Lent by the artist. Ill. p. 46

Painting (Number 2). 1960. Oil on canvas, 18⅛″ x 13″. Lent by the artist. Ill. p. 46

ANTONI TÀPIES

Painter. Born Barcelona, 1923. In 1946 abandoned study of law at University of Barcelona to devote himself full-time to painting. Self-taught. Co-founder, with painters Tharrats, Ponç, and Cuixart and writers Brossa, Puig and Cirlot of *Dau Al Set,* Barcelona, 1948. First one-man show, Galerías Layetanas, Barcelona, 1950. In the same year won French Government fellowship for sojourn in France. Traveled to Belgium and The Netherlands, 1951. Upon return to Spain, participated in the first official *Dau Al Set* exhibition in Barcelona, 1951. Came to New York, 1953, for first one-man show in the United States, Martha Jackson Gallery, New York. First one-man show in Paris, Galerie Stadler, 1955. Included in the following international exhibitions: Pittsburgh International Exhibition of Contemporary Painting, 1950, 1952, 1955; Bienal Hispanoamericana, Madrid, 1951, Havana (Cuba), 1953 and Barcelona, 1955; Venice Biennale, 1952, 1954, 1958 (won David E. Bright prize); Premio Lissone, Lissone (Italy), 1957; São Paulo Bienal, 1953 (won Acquisition Prize), 1957; Pittsburgh Bicentennial International Exhibition of Painting and Sculpture, 1958-59 (won First Prize, Painting). Shown in London, in *La Nueva Pintura de España,* 1960.[3] In the United States, participated in *European Art Today,* Minneapolis, 1959,[2] and in *Recent Acquisitions,* The Museum of Modern Art, New York, 1959. Lives in Barcelona.

Space. 1956. Latex paint with marble dust on canvas, 76⅝″ x 67″. The Museum of Modern Art, gift of Mrs. Martha Jackson. Ill. p. 49

Graffiti on Blackish Ochre Relief. 1957. Mixed media on canvas, 25″ x 32½″. Lent by Mr. and Mrs. Morton G. Neumann, Chicago, Ill. p. 48

Painting. 1957. Latex paint with marble dust and sand on canvas, 57⅜″ x 35″. The Museum of Modern Art, gift of G. David Thompson. Frontispiece

Three Stains on Grey Space. 1957. Mixed media on canvas, 57½″ x 35⅛″. Lent by Miss Isabel C. Raphael, New York. Ill. p. 47

**Reddish Painting.* 1958. Mixed media on canvas, 51¼″ x 51¼″. Lent by Martha Jackson Gallery, New York. Ill. p. 49

JOAN JOSEP THARRATS

Painter. Born Gerona, 1918. Studied in Beziers, France, 1931-33. Settled with his family in Barcelona in 1935; attended Escuela Massana, 1935-36. Traveled to Morocco, 1941. First abstract paintings, 1946. In 1948 with painters Tàpies, Ponç and Cuixart and writers Brossa, Puig and Cirlot, founded the *Dau Al Set* group, Barcelona. Went to Paris, 1949. First one-man show, Galerías El Jardín, Barcelona, 1950. Participated in the first official exhibition of the *Dau Al Set* group in 1951, Sala Caralt, Barcelona. In 1953, received fellowship from the Institut Français for a sojourn in Paris. Has designed costumes and scenery for the ballet and among his commissions is a large mural in the Church of Hogares de Mundet, Barcelona, 1957. First one-man show (collages) in the United States, Wittenborn and Co., New York, 1955. Among the international exhibitions in which he has participated are: Bienal Hispanoamericana, Madrid, 1951 and Barcelona, 1955; Venice Biennale, 1956, 1958, 1960; Biennial of Mediterranean Art, Alexandria (Egypt), 1957; São Paulo Bienal, 1959. Included in *13 peintres espagnols actuels,* Paris, 1959[1] and *La Nueva Pintura de España,* London, 1960.[3] Lives in Barcelona.

Médamothi. 1958-60. Oil on canvas, 44⅞" x 79¾". Lent by the artist. Ill. p. 50

Homage to Frank Lloyd Wright. 1959. Oil on canvas, 63¾" x 51¼". Lent by Mme Alexis Zalstem-Zalessky, New Milford, Connecticut. Ill. p. 51

Sign. 1959. Oil on canvas, 39⅜" x 39⅜". Lent by Rear Admiral Paul Lamar Joachim (U.S.N., retired), Chicago. Ill. p. 50

MANUEL VIOLA.

Painter. Born Saragossa, 1919. In 1934, first came in contact with *Adlan* group ("l'amics de l'art nou"), in Barcelona. Lived in Paris, 1939-49, where he exhibited in many group shows. 1945-49 participated in exhibitions under the name of "Manuel." From 1948 to 1953 did not exhibit. First one-man show in Madrid, 1953. First one-man show abroad, Galerie Claude Bernard, Paris, 1957. In 1958, invited by members of the *El Paso* group to join in their exhibitions. Participated in the following international exhibitions: Premio Lissone, Lissone (Italy), 1959; São Paulo Bienal, 1959. Included in *13 peintres espagnols actuels,* Paris, 1959.[1] Lives in Madrid.

The Arrow. 1958. Oil on canvas, 63¾" x 38⅞". Lent by the artist. Ill. p. 52

Homage to Rothko. 1959. Oil on canvas, 51¼" x 35¾". Lent by Walter S. Goodhue, Alexandria, Virginia. Ill. p. 53

SELECTIVE BIBLIOGRAPHY

by Bernard Karpel
Librarian, The Museum of Modern Art

The following bibliography is limited in coverage owing to the confines of space. Researchers are urged to consult the numerous general and individual bibliographies cited below. As a result of the cooperation of Mr. González Robles and the invaluable assistance of Mr. Joan-Josep Tharrats, the Library has undertaken a compilation of contemporary data on the current scene (bibl. 14) which is also accessible by photostat and microfilm. Technical assistance rendered by Miss Sylvia Hill is gratefully acknowledged.

BOOKS, SERIES, etc.

1 APOLLONIO, UMBRO. Spain. *In* Art Since 1945. p. 121-124 ill. New York, Abrams, 1958. *Also German and Italian editions.*

2 CIRICI-PELLICER, ALEXANDRE. El Arte Modernista Catalán. 475 p. ill. (col. pl.) Barcelona, Aymá [c.1951]. *Stylistic background since 1900; the moderns briefly.*

3 CIRICI-PELLICER, ALEXANDRE. La Pintura Catalana. v. 2, p. 156-163 Palma de Mallorca, Ed. Moll, 1959. *On "la plàstica de l'energia: lo postguerra."*

4 CIRLOT, JUAN-EDUARDO. Arte Contemporáneo. p. 165-168 ill. Barcelona, E.D.H.A.S.A., 1958. *On "Tàpies y la pintura informalista en España." Also forthcoming: Arte del Siglo XX (Ars Hispaniae).*

5 CIRLOT, JUAN-EDUARDO. El Arte Otro. p. 104-127 ill. Barcelona, Seix y Barral, 1957. *On Tàpies, Saura, Millares, Cuixart. Bibliography.*

6 CIRLOT, JUAN-EDUARDO. Cubismo y Figuración. p. 100-105 ill. Barcelona, Seix y Barral, 1957. *On "Análisis del tachismo" (Cuixart, Saura, Tàpies). For "Magicismo plástico" see his: Diccionario de los Ismos. p. 214-215 Barcelona, Argos, 1949 (2.ed., 1956).*

7 CIRLOT, JUAN-EDUARDO. La Escultura del Siglo XX. p. 44-48 ill. Barcelona, Omega, 1956. *Bibliography.*

8 CIRLOT, JUAN-EDUARDO. Informalismo. p. 37-47 ill. (col. pl.) Barcelona, Omega, 1959. *On Tàpies, Barcelona, "El Paso", etc. Supplemented by: Ideologiá del Informalismo.* [13] *p. Valencia, Cuadernos de Arte del Movimiento Artístico del Mediterráneo, 1960.*
COLECCIÓN CUADERNOS DE ARTE. Madrid, Ateneo de Madrid, 1957-current. See bibl. 52, 63, 66, 72, 73, 78, 88, 91.
COLECCIÓN DEL ARTE DE HOY. Madrid, 1958-current. *See bibl. 62, 67, 77, 89.*

9 COURTHION, PIERRE. L'Art Indépendant. p. 182, 228 Paris, Michel, 1958. *Briefly notes Feito and Tàpies.*

10 GAYA-NUÑO, ANTONIO. Escultura Española Contemporanea. 150 p. ill. Madrid, Guadarrama, 1957.

Covers Chillida and Oteiza. Bibliography. Supplemented by: La Pintura Española del Medio Siglo. 78 p. ill. (col. pl.) Barcelona, Omega, 1952.

11 GIMÉNEZ-PLACER, FERNANDO. Historia del Arte Español. v. 2, p. 949-1042 ill. Barcelona, Ed. Labor, 1955. *Includes sections on modern painting and sculpture by Alexandre Cirici-Pellicer.*

12 GUDIOL, JOSÉ & CIRLOT, JUAN-EDUARDO. L'Art Contemporain en Espagne. *In* Encyclopédie de l'Art International Contemporain. p. 105-112 ill. Paris, Prisme des Arts, 1958.

13 MODERN ARTISTS IN AMERICA: First Series. Edited by Robert Motherwell, Ad Reinhardt, Bernard Karpel. p. 157-164 ill. New York, Wittenborn, Schultz [1951]. *From the "Dau Al Set", Barcelona.*

14 NEW YORK. MUSEUM OF MODERN ART. LIBRARY. [Archive of Spanish Artists]. New York [1960]. *A continuing collection (in folio) of biographical and bibliographical notes, reviews and clippings, typescripts and photographs, etc. which already includes data on Farreras, Millares, Rivera, Saura, Serrano, Suárez, Tharrats, Viola and others.*

15 OTEIZA, JORGE DE OTEIZA EMBIL. Interpretación Estética de la Estatuaria Megalítica Americana. Madrid, Ed. Cultura Hispanica, 1952.

16 READ, HERBERT. A Concise History of Modern Painting. p. 270, 276, 289, 329 ill. New York, Praeger, 1959.

17 RODRÍGUEZ-AGUILERA, CESÁREO. Antología Española de Arte Contemporáneo. p. 93-94, 97-98, 117-118, 123-124 ill. Barcelona, Barna, 1955.

18 SAURA, ANTONIO. Arte Fantastico. [7] p. plus 14 plates Madrid, Libreria Clan [1953]. *Colección Artistas Nuevos, 12. . . . "para conmemorar la exposición."*

19 SEUPHOR, MICHEL. Dictionary of Abstract Painting. p. 75, 171 ill. New York, Paris Book Center, 1957. *Also Paris, Hazan, 1957. Includes Feito, Tàpies.*

20 SEUPHOR, MICHEL. The Sculpture of This Century. p. 182-183, 251, 312, 331 ill. New York, Braziller, 1960. *Biographies on Chillida, Oteiza, Serrano. Translated from the French (Ed. Griffon, 1959).*

JOURNALS & SPECIAL NOS.

21 AUJORD'HUI (Boulogne-sur-Seine) No. 24, Dec. 1959. *On "La peinture espagnole d'aujourd'hui" with texts by M. Conde, J. Ayllon, J.-E. Cirlot, J.-M. Moreno Galvan. Also "La sculpture abstraite espagnole" by V. Aguilera-Cerni. Illustrated.*

22 DAU AL SET (Barcelona). 1948-195? *Founded by J.-J. Tharrats in association with Joan Brossa, M. Cuixart, Joan Ponç, Arnald Puig, A. Tàpies, who along with others, variously edited and illustrated this graphic "revista". Numerous critiques and exhibition notices, reproductions of works and illustrations by the Barcelona circle, special numbers and lead articles.*

23 LA ISLA DE LOS RATONES (Santander) No. 16-17, Feb. 1952. *On "Pintura catalana contemporánea" with main*

article by C. Rodríguez-Aguilera. *Extraordinary limited issue published in 90 copies. Illustrated.*

24   LOS PAPELES DE SON ARMADANS (Palma de Mallorca). No. 37, April 1959. *Cover-title: "El Paso". Articles by J.-E. Cirlot, A. Saura, M. Viola, R. Canogar, M. Rivera, M. Chirino, M. Millares, L. Feito. Illustrated.*

25   REVISTA DE ACTUALIDADES ARTES Y LETRAS (Barcelona). 1957-current. *Includes weekly articles by Joan-Josep Tharrats as well as a special series, e.g. "Artistas de Hoy" (1957-1959) including Tàpies, Millares, Serrano, Saura, Cuixart, Canogar, Feito, Suárez, etc. Illus.*

ARTICLES

26   CHOAY, FRANÇOISE. L'école espagnole. *L'Oeil* (Paris) no. 51: 10-17 ill. (col.) Mar. 1959. *On "Dau Al Set" and "El Paso", etc.*

27   CIRLOT, JUAN-EDUARDO. N.É.É.: l'apport espagnol à la nouvelle école européenne. *Art Actuel International* (Lausanne) no. 15: [3] ill. 1960. *Artists in Barcelona and Madrid.*

28   CIRLOT, JUAN-EDUARDO. La pittura informale in Spagna. *L'Esperienza Moderna* (Rome) no. 5: 10-12 ill. Mar. 1959. *The "Dau Al Set".*

29   FAHLSTRÖM, ÖYVIND. Steget och tärningens sjunde sida. *Paletten* (Stockholm) no. 2: 40-45 ill. 1959. *On the "Dau Al Set" group.*

30   GASCH, SEBASTIÁN. El arte en Barcelona. *Ver y Estimar* (Buenos Aires) 3 no. 9: 39-44 ill. Apr. 1949. *"La vida artística . . . en las exposiciones . . ."*

31   GASCH, SEBASTIÁN. Non-representational art in Spain. *Magazine of Art* (New York) 43: 89-91 ill. Mar. 1950.

32   GAYA-NUÑO, ANTONIO. Medio siglo de movimientos vanguardistas en nuestra pintura. *Dau Al Set* (Barcelona) [20] p. ill. Dec. 1950. *Special number.*

33   GONZÁLEZ ROBLES, LUIS. Une nouvelle définition naîtra au cours des prochaines années . . . *Art Actuel International* (Lausanne) no. 15: [1] 1960.

34   GULLÓN, RICARDO. La joven pintura española. *Ver y Estimar* (Buenos Aires) 8 no. 27: 25-28, 33 Apr. 1952.

35   MOLLEDA, MERCÉDES. Chronique espagnole. *Art Actuel International* (Lausanne) no. 14 ill. 1960. *First issue of regular column on art news from Spain.*

36   POPOVICI, CIRLO L. L'art abstrait en Espagne. *Cimaise* (Paris) 3 no. 1: 7-9 ill. Oct.-Nov. 1955. *English résumé, p. 3-4.*

37   REICHARDT, JASIA. New Spanish painting. *Art News and Review* (London) 12 no. 1: 5 ill. Jan. 30, 1960. *Also comments on Tooth exhibition (bibl. 51).*

38   RESTANY, PIERRE. La jeune peinture espagnole rentre en scène. *Cimaise* (Paris) no. 45-46: 66-79 ill. (col.) Sept.-Nov. 1959. *Text also in English, German, Spanish.*

39   ROH, FRANZ. Junge spanische Malerei. *Das Kunstwerk* (Baden-Baden) no. 7:13-14 Jan. 1960. *Includes brief statements; illus., p. 15-21; English summary opp. p. 1.*

40   SÖDERBERG, LASSE. À Barcelone et à Madrid: peinture et vérité. *Cahiers du Musée de Poche* (Paris) no. 2: 63-66, 73-74 ill. June 1959.

41   SERPAN, IAROSLAV. D'ailleurs et de mille part (Espagne). *Le Soleil Noir* (Paris) no. 3-4: 194 1953. *Special number ed. by R. Lebel: Premier Bilan de l'Art Actuel, 1937-1953.*

42   THARRATS, JOAN-JOSEP. Plein essor de l'art abstrait en Espagne. *Art Actuel International* (Lausanne) no. 4: [6] 1958. *Also mentions Spanish awards at the Venice Biennale, 1958.*

43   THARRATS, JOAN-JOSEP. [Weekly column on art]. *Revista* (Barcelona) 1957-current. *See bibl. 25.*

44   WESCHER, HERTA. Les participations espagnole et yougoslave à la XXIXe biennale de Venise. *Quadrum* (Brussels) no. 6: 51-68 ill. 1959. *English résumé, p. 200-201.*

45   WRETHOLM, EUGEN. Unga spanjorer. *Konstrevy* (Stockholm) no. 1: 34, 36 ill. 1960.

CATALOGS

46   ASCHAFFENBURG. GALERIE 59. Arte Actuel: Zeitgenössische Spanische Kunst. [32] p. ill. Aschaffenburg, 1960. *Exhibits in all media; biographies, bibliography; texts by W. E. Simmat and J.-E. Cirlot, including his essay on Serrano's sculpture (bibl. 90).*

47   BARCELONA. SALA GASPAR. Otro Arte: Exposicion Internacional de Pintura y Escultura. [14] p. ill. Barcelona, 1957. *In association with the "Club 49" (Barcelona) and the Galerie Stadler (Paris); preface by Michel Tapié; biographical notes on Saura, Tàpies, Tharrats. Shown, with modifications, at Madrid.*

48   BARCELONA. BIENAL HISPANOAMERICANA DE ARTE. Catalogo Oficial. Barcelona, 1955-current. *Includes representation of the young Spaniards, with varying texts, e.g. 1955 by L. F. Vivanco, etc.*

49   KASSEL. MUSEUM FRIDERICIANUM. II. Documenta '59: Kunst nach 1945, Internationale Ausstellung. 3 vol. ill. Cologne, DuMont Schauberg, 1959. *Spanish artists in v. 1, 2; biographical and bibliographical notes; texts by W. Haftmann and E. Trier.*

50   LISSONE. PREMIO LISSONE, XI. Catalogo. [40] p. ill. Lissone, 1959. *International exhibit of painting; Spanish section includes biographies; preface by C. G. Argan (also published in "I 4 Soli".)*

51   LONDON. ARTHUR TOOTH & SONS. La Nueva Pintura de España: Ten Contemporary Spanish Painters. [24] p. ill. London, 1960. *Biographical notes on Cuixart, Feito, Millares, Saura, Tàpies, Tharrats, etc.; preface by J.-E. Cirlot (p. 3-9).*

52   MADRID. ATENEO DE MADRID. Colección Cuadernos de Arte. Madrid, 1957-current. *Illustrated booklets for shows in Madrid, Barcelona, etc. Issued 1957: Serrano, Millares, Canogar.-1958: Muñoz, Chirino.-1959: Rivera, Farreras, Suárez.*

53 MADRID. GALERIA BUCCHOLZ. El Paso. [8] p. Madrid, 1957. *"Primera exposición del grupo"—Canogar, Feito, Frances, Millares, Rivera, Saura, Serrano, Suárez. Brief statement also in French, German, English, Arabic.*

54 MADRID. [GRUPO "EL PASO"]. Cuatro Pintores Españoles. [12] p. ill. Madrid, 1958. *Biographies and statements by Canogar, Feito, Millares, Saura. French text inserted. Also shown at Barcelona, 1959.*

55 MINNEAPOLIS. INSTITUTE OF ARTS. European Art Today: 35 Painters and Sculptors. 88 p. ill. Minneapolis, 1959. *Exhibit shown in U.S. and Canada; biographies of Canogar, Chillida, Saura, Tàpies; text by J.-E. Cirlot and S. Hunter.*

56 NEW YORK. PIERRE MATISSE GALLERY. Millares, Canogar, Rivera, Saura. [32] p. ill. New York, 1960. *Biographies and statements; preface by J.-E. Cirlot on the "El Paso" circle.*

57 PARIS. MUSÉE DES ARTS DÉCORATIFS. 13 Peintres Espagnols Actuels. [40] p. ill. Paris, 1959. *Introduction by J.-M. Ruiz Morales; biographical notes; bibliography. Also shown at Fribourg (Musée d'Art et d'Histoire), Basel (Kunsthalle), The Hague (Gemeentemuseum), Amsterdam (Stedelijk Museum), Munich (Akademie für Bautechnik). Similarly modified catalogs and exhibits in 1960 for Göteborg and Oslo.*

58 PITTSBURGH. CARNEGIE INSTITUTE. Bicentennial International Exhibition of Contemporary Painting and Sculpture. Pittsburgh, 1958. *Exhibited Dec. 1958-Feb. 1959; Spanish section included Canogar, Chillida, Cuixart, Saura, Tàpies; occasional representation in previous internationals.*

59 RIO DE JANEIRO. MUSEU DE ARTE MODERNA. Espaço e Cor na Pintura Espanhola de Hoje. [80] p. ill. Rio de Janeiro, 1959. *Texts by J.-M. Ruiz Morales, C. Fléxa Ribeiro, L. González Robles; biographical notes. Also at the Museu de Arte Moderna (São Paulo), 1960.*

60 SÃO PAULO. BIENAL DO MUSEU DE ARTE MODERNA. Catálogo Geral. São Paulo, 1951-current. *Includes Spanish representation (2d, 4th, 5th biennial); texts by L. González Robles, J. R. Masoliver, etc. Frequently reviewed, e.g. A. Cirici-Pellicer, Revista (Barcelona), 8 no. 393: 12-13 Oct. 24, 1959.*

61 VENICE. ESPOSICION BIENAL INTERNACIONAL DE ARTE, XXIX. Artistas Espanoles. [50] p. ill. Venice, 1958. *Catalog of the Spanish Pavilion; preface by L. González Robles; artists' biographies. Spanish sections also included in recent biennial catalogs (1952, 1954, 1956, etc.), with texts and notes. The latest Biennale (XXX, 1960) is also organized by Mr. Luis González Robles.*

PAINTERS

Catalogs recorded above include supplemental documentation on most of the artists listed here. *Bibliographies,* where mentioned, provide additional references not possible to record on this occasion. Note also *general*

citations, e.g. "Dau Al Set" (bibl. 22), and, in particular, bibl. 32.

Canogar, Rafael

62 CRISPOLTI, ENRICO. Rafael Canogar. [12] p. ill. Madrid, Arte de Hoy, 1959. *Colección del Arte de Hoy, no. 4; bibliography. Supplemented by his catalog for Galeria Blu (Milan) Nov. 30, 1959.*

63 FERNANDEZ DEL AMO, JOSÉ LUIS. Canogar al Espectador. [32] p. ill. Madrid, Ateneo de Madrid, 1957. *Cuadernos de Arte, no. 20; published for March show at Ateneo Barcelones.*

Cuixart, Modest

64 CIRLOT, JUAN-EDUARDO. La Peinture de Modest Cuixart. [121] p. incl. ill. (col. pl.) Barcelona, Galerie Jardin & Paris, Galerie René Drouin, 1958. *"Édition dirigée par René P. Métras . . . mai-juin 1958." Texts by R. Drouin, J. J. Lerrant, R. P. Métras, extensive bibliography, résumés in Spanish and English. Cirlot's essay (28 p.) is complemented by articles in "Art Actuel International" no. 7 (1959), no. 10 (1959-60).*

65 MODEST CUIXART. Dau Al Set (Barcelona) [22] p. incl. ill. Spring 1955. *Critiques by Alexandre Cirici-Pellicer and Joan Brossa.*

Farreras, Francisco

66 FISAC, MIGUEL. *Francisco Farreras.* [10] p. ill. Madrid, Ateneo de Madrid, 1959. *Cuadernos de Arte, no. 48, issued for May exhibition.*

67 TAFUR, JOSÉ LUIS. Francisco Farreras. [16] p. ill. Madrid, Arte de Hoy, 1960. *Collección del Arte de Hoy, no. 6; text also in French, bibliography.*

Feito, Luis

68 BOUDAILLE, GEORGES. A la découverte de Luis Feito. Cimaise (Paris) 5 no. 4: 24-25 ill. Mar.-Apr. 1958. *English translation, p. 9-10.*

69 RESTANY, PIERRE. Feito. 94 p. ill. (col. pl.) Paris, Galerie Arnaud [1960]. *Text, dated Nov. 1959, also in English and Spanish; biographical and bibliographical notes. Special edition (25 copies) with an original gouache. Essay by Restany also published in "Art International", no. 1-2, 1959.*

Millares, Manolo

70 AGUILERA-CERNI, VINCENTE. Millares. [11] p. ill. [Madrid, n.d.] *Text dated 1957; bibliography. Also essay in "I 4 Soli", no. 4, July-Aug. 1959.*

71 MATISSE, PIERRE, GALLERY. Manolo Millares: Recent Paintings, April 12-May 7. [20] p. incl. ill. (port.) New York, 1960. *Artist's statement, biographical note, lists 15 works.*

(Muñoz), Lucio

72 OIZA, FRANCISCO SAENZ. Lucio Muñoz. [10] p. ill. Madrid, Ateneo de Madrid, 1958. *Cuadernos de Arte, no. 39, published for Dec. exhibit at the Ateneo.*

Rivera, Manuel

73 GONZÁLEZ ROBLES, LUIS. Manuel Rivera. [77] p. plus 10 plates. Madrid, Ateneo del Madrid, 1959. *Cuadernos de Arte, no. 42. Published for exhibit at the Ateneo (Feb.-Mar).*

74 AROSTEGUI, ANTONIO. Rivera, un Pintor Granadino. Granada, Patria, 1957. *Also "Manuel Rivera", (1952).*

Saura, Antonio

75 BOMAN, ERIK. Saura. [18] p. ill. [Madrid, 1956]. *French text dated "Paris, Nov. 1955"; published for exhibit at El Palacio de Bibliotecas y Museos de Madrid (Feb. 1956).*

76 ODYSSIA, GALLERIA. Antonio Saura. [11] p. ill. Rome, 1960. *Preface by Michel Tapié for February exhibit.*

Suárez, Antonio

77 CASTRO ARINES, JOSÉ DE. El Pintor Antonio Suárez. [11] p. plus 14 ill. Madrid, Arte de Hoy, 1959. *Colección del Arte de Hoy, no. 2.*

78 CIRLOT, JUAN-EDUARDO. Antonio Suárez. [12] p. ill. Madrid, Ateneo de Madrid, 1959. *Published for Oct.- Nov. exhibit at the Ateneo; Cuadernos de Arte, no. 52.*

Tàpies, Antoni

79 CIRLOT, JUAN-EDUARDO. La Pintura de Antonio Tàpies. [Madrid—Palma de Mallorca, 1958]. *Limited edition of 50 copies of essay originally published in "Papeles de Son Armadans", no. 26: 203-207 May 1958. Additional text in his "El Arte Otro", p. 104-110 (bibl. 5), and "Informalismo", p. 37-41 (bibl. 8).*

80 TAPIÉ, MICHEL. Antonio Tàpies. Selección y secuencia, J. Prats-Vallés. [15] p. plus 51 plates (pt. col.) Barcelona, Editorial R M, 1959. *Works photographed by J. P.-V.; text also in English and French. Also by Tapié: Antonio Tàpies et l'oeuvre complète. [40] p. Barcelona, Dau Al Set, 1955.*

81 THARRATS, JOAN-JOSEP. Antonio Tàpies o el Dau Modern de Versailles. [24] p. ill. Barcelona, Dau Al Set, 1950. *Published for first exhibition, Oct. 1950; biographical and bibliographical notes.*

Tharrats, Joan-Josep

82 NEW YORK. MUSEUM OF MODERN ART. LIBRARY. [Documents on J.-J. Tharrats]. 1960. *A cumulative file of catalogs, clippings, reviews, photos, writings and bibliography (mounted folio). Of special importance: J.-J. Tharrats—Collages, Maculatures—"Dau Al Set", Estiu de 1954 (Limited signed edition, with originals).*

—Tharrats, 1955—"Dau Al Set", Estiu 1955 (Text by C. Rodríguez-Aguilera; biography and bibliography).

83 [SARTORIS, ALBERTO & CIRLOT, JUAN-EDUARDO]. Las Maculaturas de Tharrats. [40] p. ill. Barcelona, 1959. *Issued for his print show at the V. Biennal, São Paulo. Biographical and bibliographical notes.*

Viola, Manuel

84 VIOLA, MANUEL. Anti-arte. *Papeles de Son Armadans (Madrid)* 4 no. 37: 67-69 Apr. 1959.

85 VIOLA, MANUEL. Hacia el "arte otro". *Cuadernas de Arte y Pensamiento (Madrid)* no. 2: 73-74, 77-78, 81 ill. Jan. 1960.

SCULPTORS

Chillida, Eduardo

86 BACHELARD, GASTON. Le Cosmos du fer. *Derrière le Miroir (Paris)* no. 90-91: [1-7] ill. Oct.-Nov. 1956. *Preface for Galerie Maeght show of 27 works by Chillida, biographical notes.*

87 SEUPHOR, MICHEL. La Sculpture de ce Siècle: Dictionnaire de la Sculpture Moderne. p. 182-183, 251, ill. Neuchâtel, Griffon, 1959. *Also American edition (Braziller, 1960).*

Chirino, Martin

88 AYLLON, JOSÉ. Los Hierros de Martin Chirino. [32] p. ill. Madrid, Ateneo de Madrid, 1958. *Cuadernos de Arte, no. 29, published for exhibit at the Ateneo (Feb.-Mar.).*

89 FERRANT, ANGEL. Martin Chirino es un Escultor [9] p. plus 20 ill. Madrid, Arte de Hoy, 1959. *Colección del Arte de Hoy, no. 3.*

Oteiza, (Jorge de Oteiza Embil)

90 [OTEIZA, JORGE DE ORTEIZA EMBIL]. ESCULPTURE . . . Catalogue: IV Biennale de São Paulo. [24] p. ill. Madrid, Graficas Reunidas, 1957. *Sept. exhibition at São Paulo, lists 28 works, includes "Propos experimental 1956-1957" and "Documentation graphique."*

91 SARTORIS, ALBERTO. Flamberge au vent. *In his* Encyclopédie de l'Architecture Nouvelle v. 3, p. 29-30 Milan, Hoepli, 1954.

Serrano, Pablo

92 CIRLOT, JUAN-EDUARDO. P. Serrano. 12 p. ill. Madrid, Galleria Silo, 1959. *Insert also in English and French: "Concepto de la forma . . ." was published in Correo de las Artes (Barcelona), 3 no. 20: 3 Oct. 1959.*

93 FERRARI, ENRIQUE LAFUENTE. Pablo Serrano: Escultor a Dos Vertientes. [32] p. ill. Madrid, Ateneo de Madrid, 1957. *Cuadernos de Arte, no. 14; published for Jan. exhibit in Barcelona.*